T·H·E
HOUSE
BOOK

A PERSONAL RECORD

[Paste a photograph of your house here]

ADDRESS ....

....

....

TELEPHONE NUMBER ....

T·H·E
HOUSE
BOOK

A PERSONAL RECORD

For a man's house is his castle.
SIR EDWARD COKE (1552–1634)

STUDIO
DESIGNS

First published in 1994 by Studio Designs,
A Division of Studio Editions Ltd.,
Princess House, 50 Eastcastle Street,
London W1N 7AP, England.

Printed in Spain

Cover illustration 'Greenhurst', Sussex
by Clive Nichols Photography © Clive Nichols

CONTENTS

INTRODUCTION

This is *your* book, unique to your home and family. Within these pages you can create an invaluable archive that reflects your very own life style and environment.

No two homes are ever alike, even if they were built at the same time and to the same design. It is the occupant who makes a house into a home; who imprints on the structure and surroundings the stamp of individuality and character.

In the pages that follow are sections where you can record the events and changes that take place in your home; the improvements and repairs you carry out; the special occasions and celebrations that you have enjoyed; and the progress of your family.

How time flies! And, before we know it, the memory has clouded the details of past events. Can you remember when last you decorated the bedrooms? And what colour they were before that? Here are pages for you to write those things down, so that they will not be lost.

This book will become not only a permanent record, but a useful reference too. There are sections where you can keep track of your gardening activities (where, for example, you planted those annual flowers), your house guests (when *did* they last visit?), and your entertaining, plus pages for jotting down a summary of each year, which will gradually build into a history of your family and home.

A living chronicle and record, this will build into a book to which you can continually return, updating, recording and savouring the pleasures of years past – a very special archive of *your* house and home.

Sydney R Jones
'19

8

1
OUR HOUSE

'Mid pleasures and palaces though we may roam,
Be it ever so humble, there's no place like home.
J. H. PAYNE (1792–1852)

HISTORY OF THE SITE AND STRUCTURE

Today, building proceeds apace, as the town and cities continue to spread into the countryside and new developments eat up green fields. In the cities, new buildings replace the old.

The Deeds of your property will tell you much about the background of your building; in the local library and museum can usually be found records of the history of the site – what it was before the house was built, and who owned it. Possibly it was part of a large estate; or part of a farm. Some beautiful dwellings have been created by conversions from barns and stables, while tiny terraced cottages are often combined to provide homes of character and charm.

Local archives will contain old maps of the district. Your neighbours too can help. Old people will be able to remember, often to the early years of the century; and they may be able to tell you fascinating details of the site and surroundings. Old photographs will help to complete the picture.

_____

_____

_____

_____

_____

_____

_____

_____

_____

_____

HISTORY OF THE SITE AND STRUCTURE

PREVIOUS OWNERS

The house in which you live, if it is an older property, will owe much to its previous occupants. It is they who will have made alterations, changes and extensions; who will have named the house; who will have decorated it; and, in many other ways, moulded the character of the building as it now stands. It will be interesting to find out what their occupations were – they may even have been persons of note or celebrity. The Deeds of the house will reveal much; and, again, local people will probably be able to fill out the details. In this respect, it is often possible to find a local historian, professional or amateur, who can tell you a great deal.

ARCHITECTURE
AND CONSTRUCTION

There are many books in which you can find out about the style and details of house architecture. In the past, authors tended to concentrate on the palaces and great houses of the rich and powerful; but in recent years, more and more good books have appeared to tell the story of popular domestic architecture – the sort of house in which the average person lives today.

If you live in an older property, you may find features from various periods, as successive owners have altered and improved the structure. These features are worth recording, photographing and preserving, for they contribute in no small way to the character of a house.

Look also at the building materials: the present availability of a wide range of stone, brick and tiles means that the fabric of a house can originate far away; before the days of modern high-speed transport, moving such heavy weights long distances was uneconomic, and materials from the immediate surrounding area were favoured. Today's brick and concrete-built houses can look superb; but local government planning authorities are very often keen to preserve the character of their area by maintaining the use of traditional local materials.

Architecture and Construction

Architecture and Construction

CONNECTIONS: ELECTRICITY, GAS, WATER, DRAINAGE

When things go wrong, be prepared! Note here the locations of fuse boxes, gas mains taps, and the stop valve and stop-cock for the mains water supply. A diagram showing the layout of the drains and access to them will also be worthwhile, so that in the event of a blockage the problem can be quickly located and dealt with. Are your water pipes and tank lagged against the cold of winter? Even if they are, you may still experience trouble in the depths of a freeze. Make notes of where the problems occur, for future reference.

_____

_____

_____

_____

_____

_____

_____

_____

_____

_____

_____

_____

_____

Connections: Electricity, Gas, Water, Drainage

CONNECTIONS: ELECTRICITY, GAS, WATER, DRAINAGE

HEATING
AND LIGHTING

Today, we take the supply of gas, electricity and oil for granted – how much colder and darker must have been the houses of our forebears! Here are pages to record running costs and the dates of major maintenance work and servicing.

Date	Item	Cost

Heating and Lighting

Date	Item	Cost

Heating and Lighting

Date	Item	Cost

ALTERATIONS, EXTENSIONS, MAINTENANCE AND REPAIRS

Large additions or alterations to your house will require the involvement of contractors and professional builders; but much can be achieved by the house owner with the proper skills and tools. Indeed, "do-it-yourself" is one of the principal leisure-time occupations of the modern age, providing an enjoyable and fulfilling pastime – as well as saving money.

Note here your activities and achievements, as you gradually improve the facilities of your home and keep the structure maintained. One can so easily lose track of when essential maintenance jobs were last done; now you can ensure that they are permanently recorded.

DATE	ITEM

ALTERATIONS, EXTENSIONS, MAINTENANCE AND REPAIRS

Date	Item

ALTERATIONS, EXTENSIONS, MAINTENANCE AND REPAIRS

Date	Item

INTERIOR DECORATION

Styles and fashions come and go; so too do products. Here are pages on which you can note the colours, specifications and materials you have used, room by room – and where you bought them – so that when you need to repair or renew them, you have instant access to the materials you need.

INTERIOR DECORATION

INTERIOR DECORATION

INDOOR PLANTS

Indoor plants add special character to a room, providing the textures and colours of nature as a refreshing counterpart to the furnishings and fabrics with which we make ourselves comfortable.

Foliage house plants provide beauty of shape and colour in their leaves, and can make a delightful feature in a room. They form a pleasant evergreen background, to which one can add the brighter colours of flowering plants, or the spiky shapes of cacti. Small trees and shrubs can contribute an interesting centrepiece.

In this section, keep a record of your successes and failures as an indoor gardener.

_____

_____

_____

_____

_____

_____

_____

_____

_____

_____

_____

_____

_____

_____

Indoor Plants

Indoor Plants

2
OUR LOCAL AREA

God made the country, and man made the town.
WILLIAM COWPER (1731–1800)

HOW TO GET HERE

When guests come to visit for the first time, you will usually be confronted with the problem of giving them directions. Here is a page on which you can sketch a map, showing the main roads from each direction, the landmarks, and the railways. This map can then be photocopied for the prospective visitor, or provide a clear guide for when you have to explain directions by telephone or letter.

A brief note of the times of the most used rail and road transport services will also be a useful reference.

LOCAL AMENITIES
AND FEATURES

As you get to know the area in which you live, you discover which shops and amenities are of most value to you and your family. Keep notes of shopping hours; of the telephone numbers of the stores you most frequently use; of the fast-food takeaways you like; of the times of services held at your local church or chapel.

LOCAL AMENITIES AND FEATURES

LOCAL AMENITIES AND FEATURES

LOCAL AMENITIES AND FEATURES

Sydney R Jones/'19

3
OUR
GARDEN

God Almighty first planted a garden;
and, indeed, it is the purest of human pleasures.
FRANCIS BACON (1561–1626)

THE SOIL
AND THE SITE

E ven the smallest garden can provide considerable pleasure for the owner. For
  many people, gardening is one of the great joys of life. It can also be a personal
haven from the stresses of the modern world.

But the uses to which you put your garden depend very much upon the
geology and topography of the site. If you are lucky enough to live in the country,
you may have good soil that can be tilled and produce vegetables, shrubs and
flowers. If you live in a town or city, you may well find that the soil is poor and full
of refuse from the construction of the house.

Before you start work on your garden, it is sensible to form an objective
assessment of the soil and the site, so that you can gauge your garden's possibilities.
Soil is, essentially, a mixture of sand, clay, chalk and humus. If you have that
balance just right, you have loam, the best of all soils for the gardener; if not, there
are many ways in which you can improve it.

Your local garden centre can supply books and materials. Keep notes here of
the qualities of your soil, and of the dressings and fertilizers you add. Make notes of
the problems you encounter and the methods by which you overcome them.

_____

_____

_____

_____

_____

_____

_____

_____

THE SOIL AND THE SITE

OUR GARDEN PLAN

Will you grow vegetables to eat or flowers and shrubs? Will you make a rock garden and grow alpine plants; or build a patio? Whatever you decide, it helps to keep a plan of your garden.

Crops need to be rotated to avoid unbalancing the nutrients in the soil, and it is worthwhile dividing your growing area into three beds. You can also keep track of the flowers you plant, and so avoid destroying them when you dig.

Drainage is an important factor in designing a garden, and it will be useful to differentiate the wetter and drier areas, so that you can adapt your planting to the prevailing conditions, or dig new draining systems.

Our Garden Plan

GROWING RECORDS: VEGETABLES

Your annual tally of crops over the years will provide an interesting record, and a useful incentive. By keeping notes of feeding and manuring, you can learn much about the potential yield of your garden.

DATE	RECORD

Growing Records: Vegetables

Date	Record

GROWING RECORDS: VEGETABLES

Date	Record

Growing Records: Vegetables

Date	Record

Growing Records: Flowers and Shrubs

Date	Record

Growing Records: Flowers and Shrubs

Date	Record

Growing Records: Flowers and Shrubs

Date	Record

GROWING RECORDS: FLOWERS AND SHRUBS

Date	Record

BIRDS AND
GARDEN WILDLIFE

Growing the right plants and shrubs will attract butterflies and bees; you can also attract birds to your garden by providing feeding and nesting facilities. In really hard weather, the provision of food in people's gardens is responsible for saving the lives of many thousands of birds.

An interesting variety of birds can be spotted in gardens, especially in gardens out of town; and exceptional weather can bring unexpected visitors. Here are pages for notes of interesting sightings.

DATE	SIGHTING

Birds and Garden Wildlife

Date	Sighting

Sydney
R. Jones
'19

4
OUR FAMILY

The generations . . . like runners
hand on the torch of life.
LUCRETIUS (99–55BC)

OUR FAMILY HISTORIES

Tracing family histories is increasingly popular today, and it can become a thoroughly absorbing hobby. Many people, by diligent research in local and national archives, can trace their ancestors back over several hundred years.

One can begin to trace a family tree quite easily by questioning parents and grandparents; and many families still keep treasured family bibles, dating back into the nineteenth century, the endpapers of which record previous generations. It is fascinating to make these family connections; and to discover the trades and occupations of one's predecessors.

Take care how you lay your family tree: the branches can very quickly overfill the page.

_____

_____

_____

_____

_____

_____

_____

_____

_____

_____

_____

OUR FAMILY TREE

OUR FAMILY HISTORIES

OUR FAMILY HISTORIES

CHILDREN: MEDICAL AND SCHOOL NOTES

As your children grow up, it is fascinating to look back at their progress, and especially pleasurable if you have kept a record. Note here how they have grown; their ailments and the vaccinations they have received; their achievements; their schools and examinations.

NAMES _____

BORN _____

_____

NAMES _____

BORN _____

_____

NAMES _____

BORN _____

_____

NAMES _____

BORN _____

_____

CHILDREN: MEDICAL AND SCHOOL NOTES

CHILDREN: MEDICAL AND SCHOOL NOTES

CHILDREN: MEDICAL AND SCHOOL NOTES

BIRTHDAYS

Why not keep track here of the gifts your relatives receive, as well as their birth dates and ages? Inspiration at present-giving time can be difficult to find!

BIRTH DATE	NAME	GIFT

BIRTHDAYS

BIRTH DATE	NAME	GIFT

BIRTHDAYS

BIRTH DATE	NAME	GIFT

SPECIAL OCCASIONS AND ANNIVERSARIES

Births, christenings, engagements, weddings, wedding anniversaries . . .

DATE	OCCASION

SPECIAL OCCASIONS AND ANNIVERSARIES

Date	Occasion

SPECIAL OCCASIONS AND ANNIVERSARIES

Date	Occasion

OUR PETS

For millions of families, the home is not complete without the family pet. But pets do not live as long as humans, and though new pets can be bought, old ones can be mourned very deeply.

These pages are for a record of the family's pets; a photograph pasted in provides a visual reminder of each.

_____

_____

_____

_____

_____

_____

_____

_____

_____

_____

_____

_____

_____

Our Pets

OUR PETS

OUR PETS

Sydney
R. Jones
'91

86

5
VISITORS

Fate chooses your relations, you choose your friends.
Sir John Denham (1615–1669)

"THE VISITORS BOOK"

Date	Name and Address

"The Visitors Book"

Date	Name and Address

"THE VISITORS BOOK"

DATE	NAME AND ADDRESS

"The Visitors Book"

Date	Name and Address

"The Visitors Book"

Date	Name and Address

"The Visitors Book"

Date	Name and Address

"The Visitors Book"

Date	Name and Address

"The Visitors Book"

Date	Name and Address

"The Visitors Book"

Date	Name and Address

ENTERTAINING

Every cook develops favourite dishes; but how easy it is to fall into the trap of serving the same menu to the same visitors on subsequent occasions. Here are pages for you to note what you served to whom, so that each time your friends come to dine you can dazzle them with the versatility of your culinary skills.

Date	Guests	Menu

Entertaining

Date	Guests	Menu

Entertaining

Date	Guests	Menu

Entertaining

Date	Guests	Menu

Entertaining

Date	Guests	Menu

Sydney
R
Jones
1911

104

6

THE DIARY OF OUR HOUSE

Time will run back, and fetch the age of gold.
JOHN MILTON (1608–1674)

THE YEARLY DIARY
OF EVENTS

JANUARY

YEAR	EVENT

FEBRUARY

YEAR	EVENT

MARCH

YEAR	EVENT

April

Year	Event

MAY

YEAR	EVENT

JUNE

YEAR	EVENT

Sydney R. Jones

JULY

YEAR	EVENT

AUGUST

YEAR	EVENT

September

Year	Event

October

Year	Event

NOVEMBER

YEAR	EVENT

December

Year	Event

7
QUICK
REFERENCE
SECTION

A house is a machine for living in.
LE CORBUSIER (1887–1965)

USEFUL NUMBERS AND ADDRESSES

TELEPHONE NO.	ADDRESS

EMERGENCY TELEPHONE NUMBERS

DOCTOR _____

POLICE _____

HOSPITAL _____

PLUMBER _____

GAS COMPANY _____

DENTIST _____

ELECTRICIAN _____

LAWYER _____

_____

_____

_____

_____

_____

_____

_____

_____

SAFETY IN THE HOME

The house can be a dangerous place. Always keep a first aid kit, and if necessary use these notes as a rapid reference.

Bleeding Check that there is nothing major in the wound, clean it if necessary, and then apply pressure to stem bleeding. It helps, if possible, to raise and support the wound. Finally apply sterile dressing or plaster.

Burns Immerse in running cold water until the pain eases.
Dry and apply a sterile dressing.
Do not apply any creams or fats.
Do not break any blisters.
Do not use plasters.
In the case of bad burns, cover the wound with a clean dressing and get assistance.
Do not try to remove charred clothing from the burn wound.

Electrocution Turn off the switch, and if possible the electricity mains. Then push or pull the victim away from the power source by a dry, non–conductive objects, such as wood, rubber or paper. If the victim is not bleeding commence artificial respiration.

Eye Injury Wash with plenty of water and try to remove any foreign bodies from the eye; if you do not succeed, leave this to expert assistance.

Choking It is vital to try to remove the obstruction from the throat/windpipe—Encourage casualty to cough, slap them between the shoulder blades, or perform abdominal thrusts.
   If breathing stops commence artificial respiration.

Fire Make one effort to put the fire out quickly; if this is impossible, evacuate the building, closing doors and windows as you leave. Call the fire service and keep back. Remember that water will not put out burning oil or fat.

Gas Gas leak—evacuate the building and call the gas company.
Asphyxiation—if gas inhaled and victim stops breathing, commence artificial respiration.

Artificial Respiration Kneel beside the casualty and look/listen for signs/sounds of breathing. If there is no sign of breathing or the casualty is unconcious and breathing is difficult, open the airway. To do this, lift the chin backwards with the thumb and index finger of one hand and gently push the forehead backwards with the other. The neck is now extended and the tongue, which may have fallen back, is pulled forward.

If breathing does not start spontaneously, quickly insert a finger in the mouth and check that no other obstruction is present, such as teeth or vomit. If breathing commences, place the casualty in the recovery position.

If the casualty is still not breathing, maintain the airway and give two breaths of your air immediately.

To do this, take a deep breath in, seal your lips to those of the casualty, with your hands pressing the forehead pinch the nose, breathe out so that you see the casualty's chest rise. Give a second breath. Now check the pulse and, if present, continue mouth to mouth respiration 12-16 times a minute.

If there is no pulse give 15 chest compressions, repeat 2 inhalations and then 15 more chest compressions . Place your hands, with fingers interlocked, on the chest and keeping the arms straight press up and down, counting, 'one, two, three'. The chest should be depressed 4-5 cm; compressions are given at the rate of 80 per minute. When breathing returns, place the casualty in the recovery position.

127